# Astro-INKLINGS

## by Tanya Bond

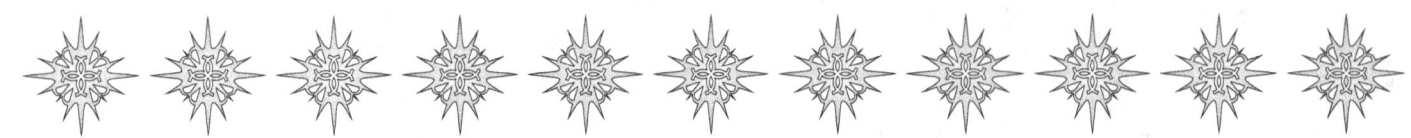

Welcome to Astro-INKLINGS colouring adventure!

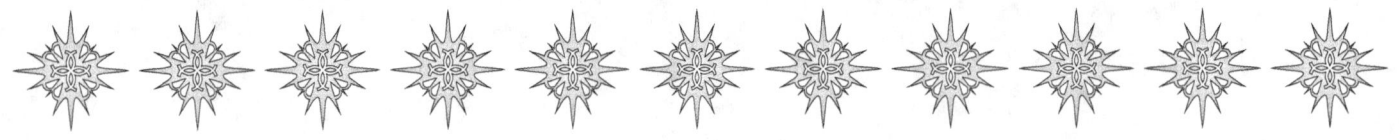

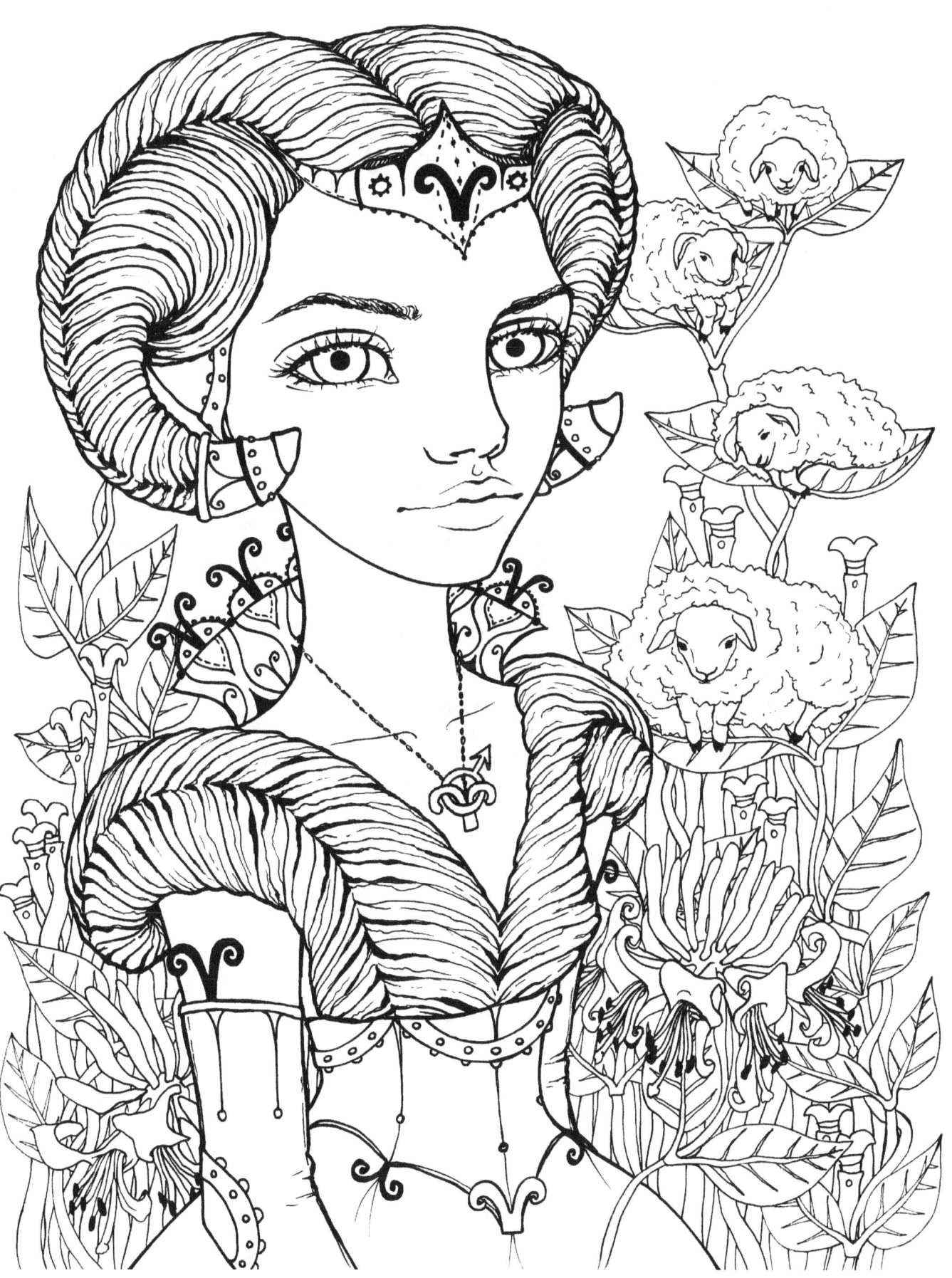

Astro-INKLINGS © Tanya Bond

♈ Aries

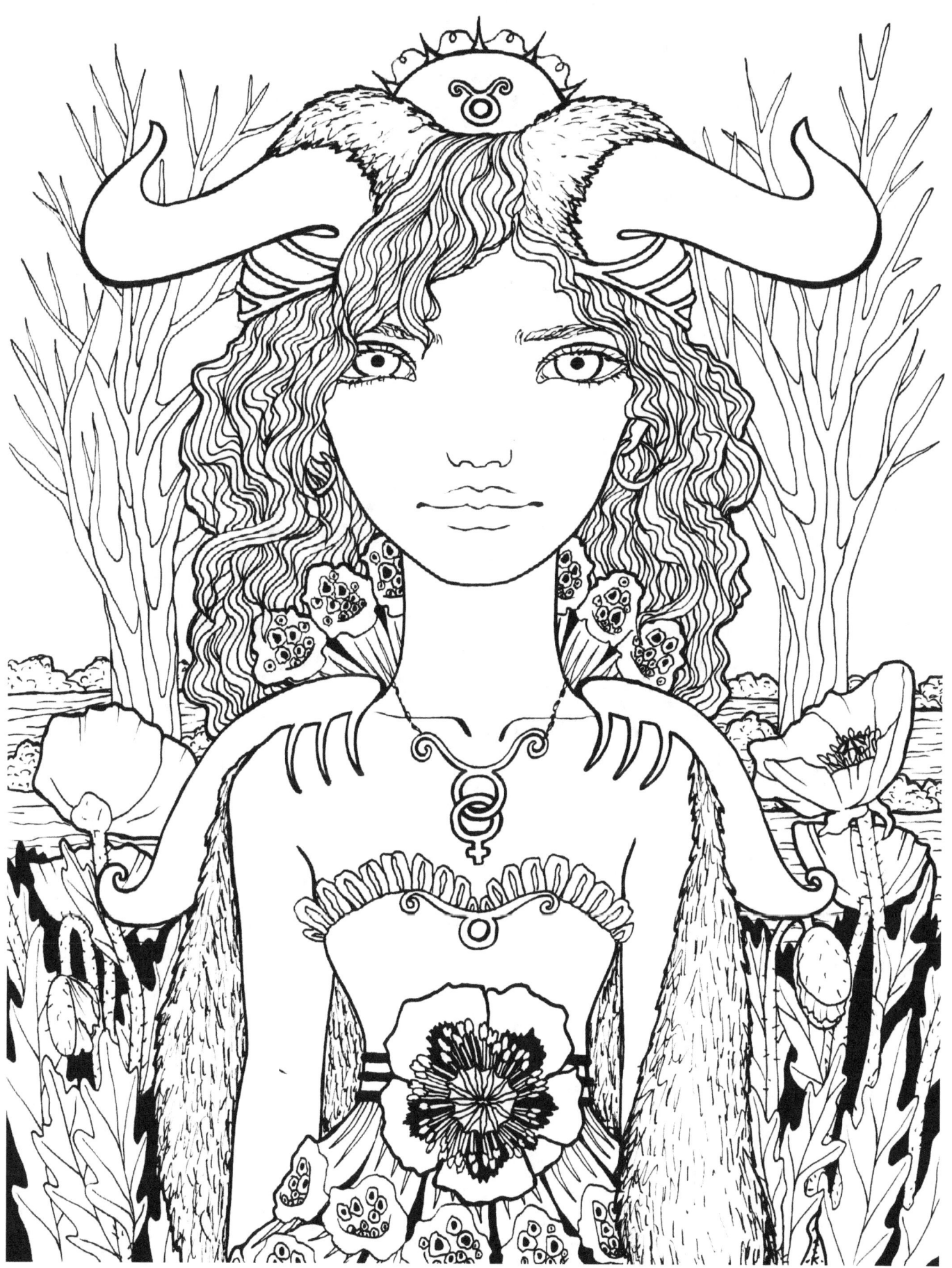

Astro-INKLINGS © Tanya Bond

♉ Taurus

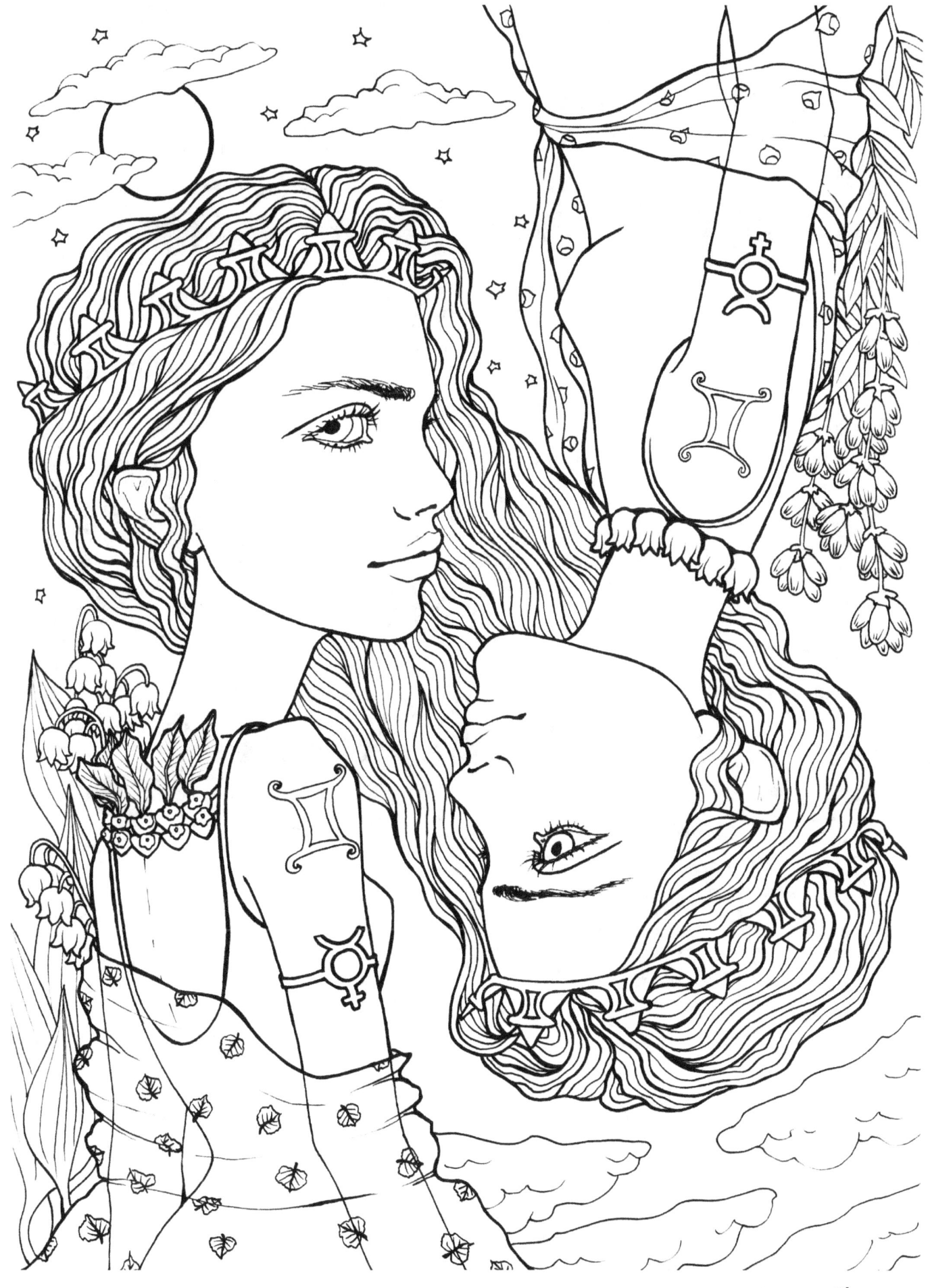

Astro-INKLINGS © Tanya Bond

♊ Gemini

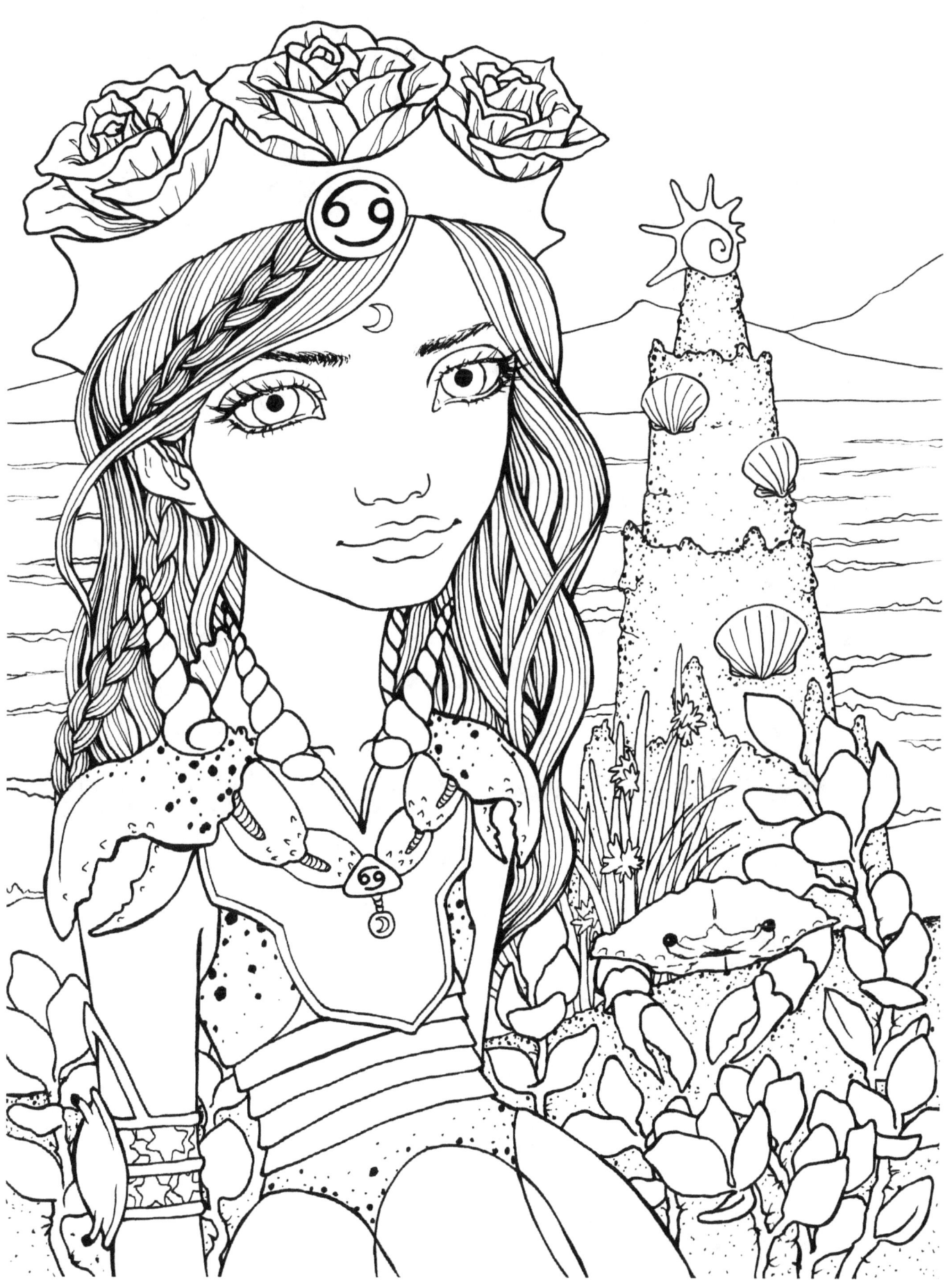

Astro-INKLINGS © Tanya Bond

♋ Cancer

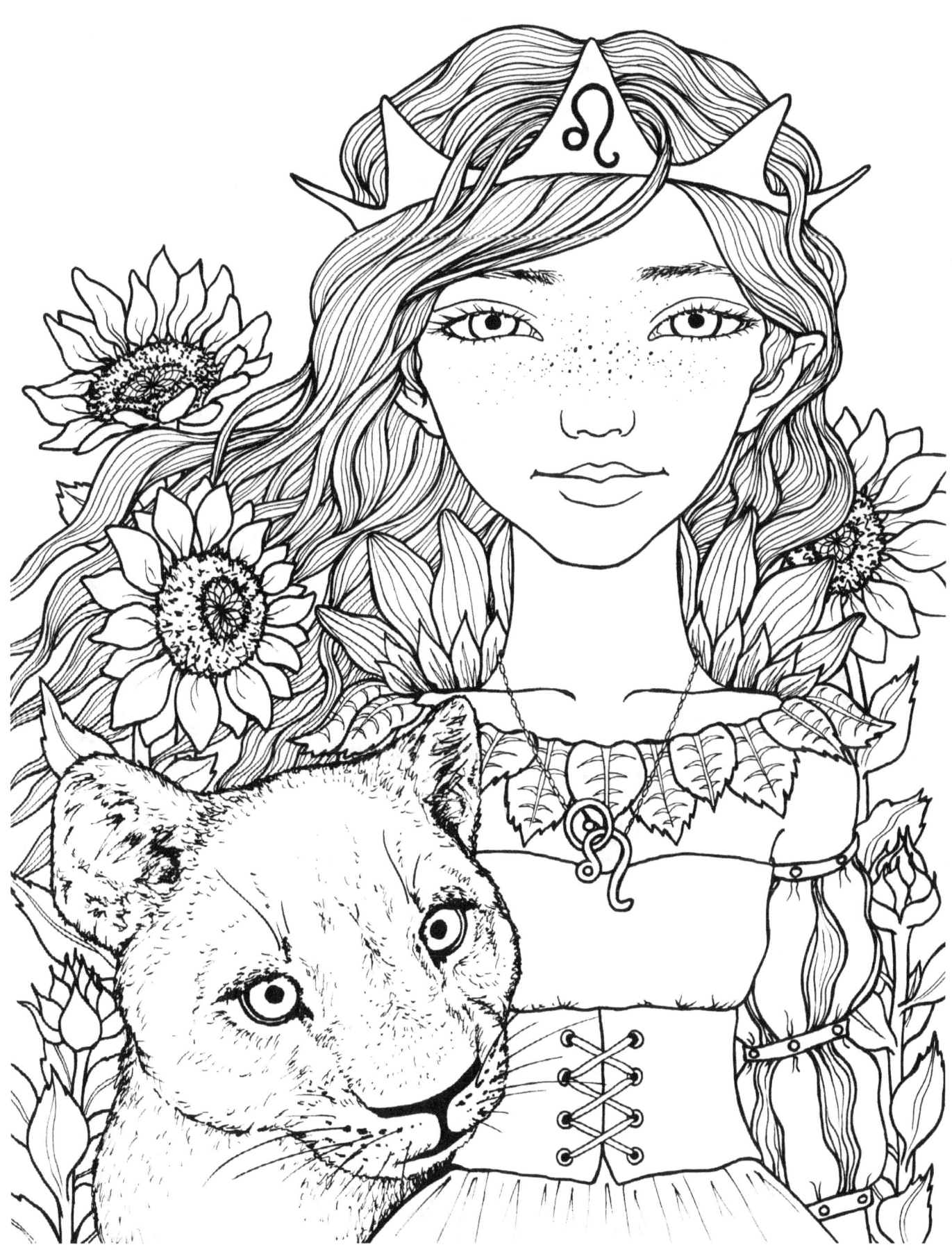

Astro-INKLINGS © Tanya Bond

♌ Leo

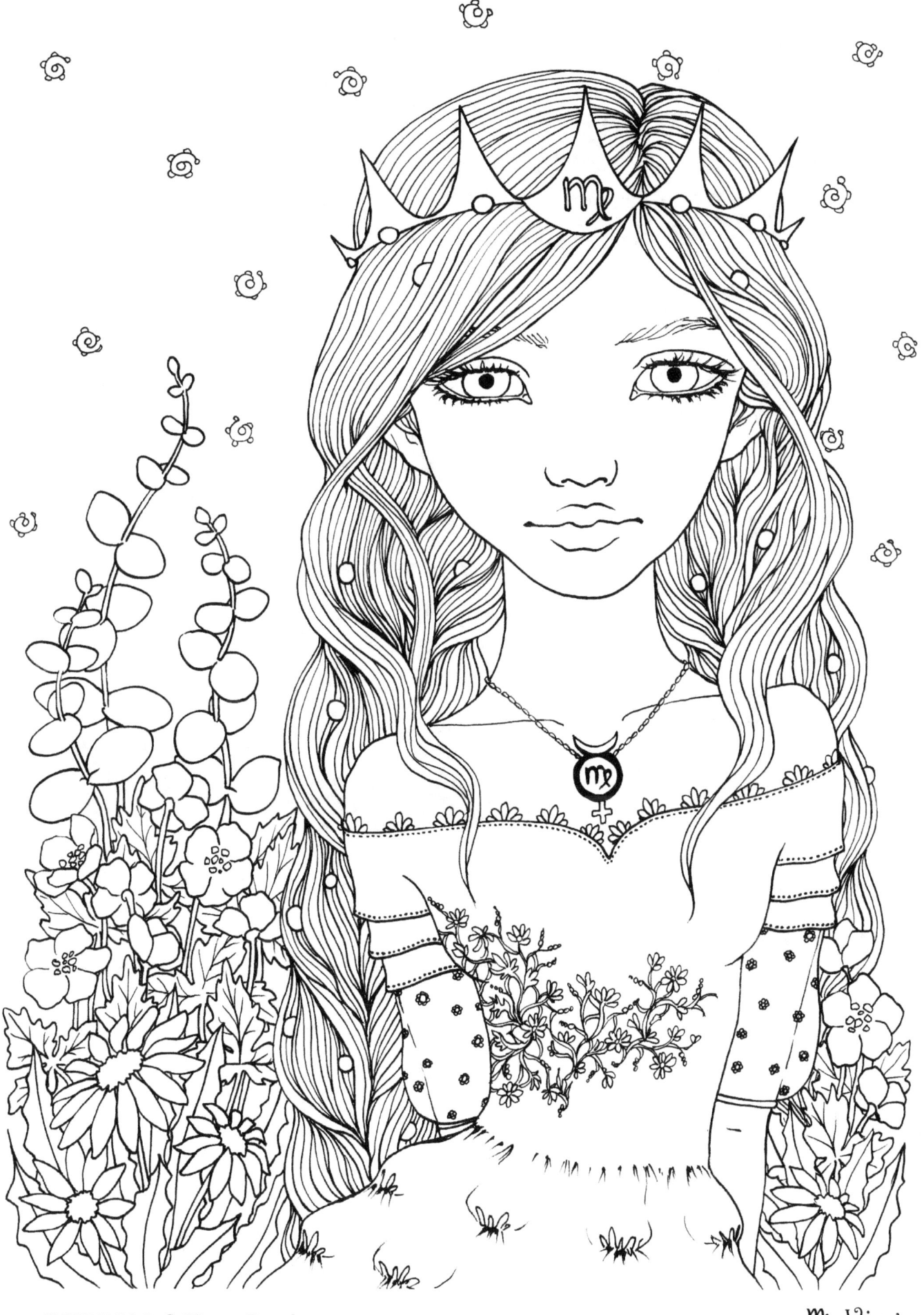

♍ Virgo

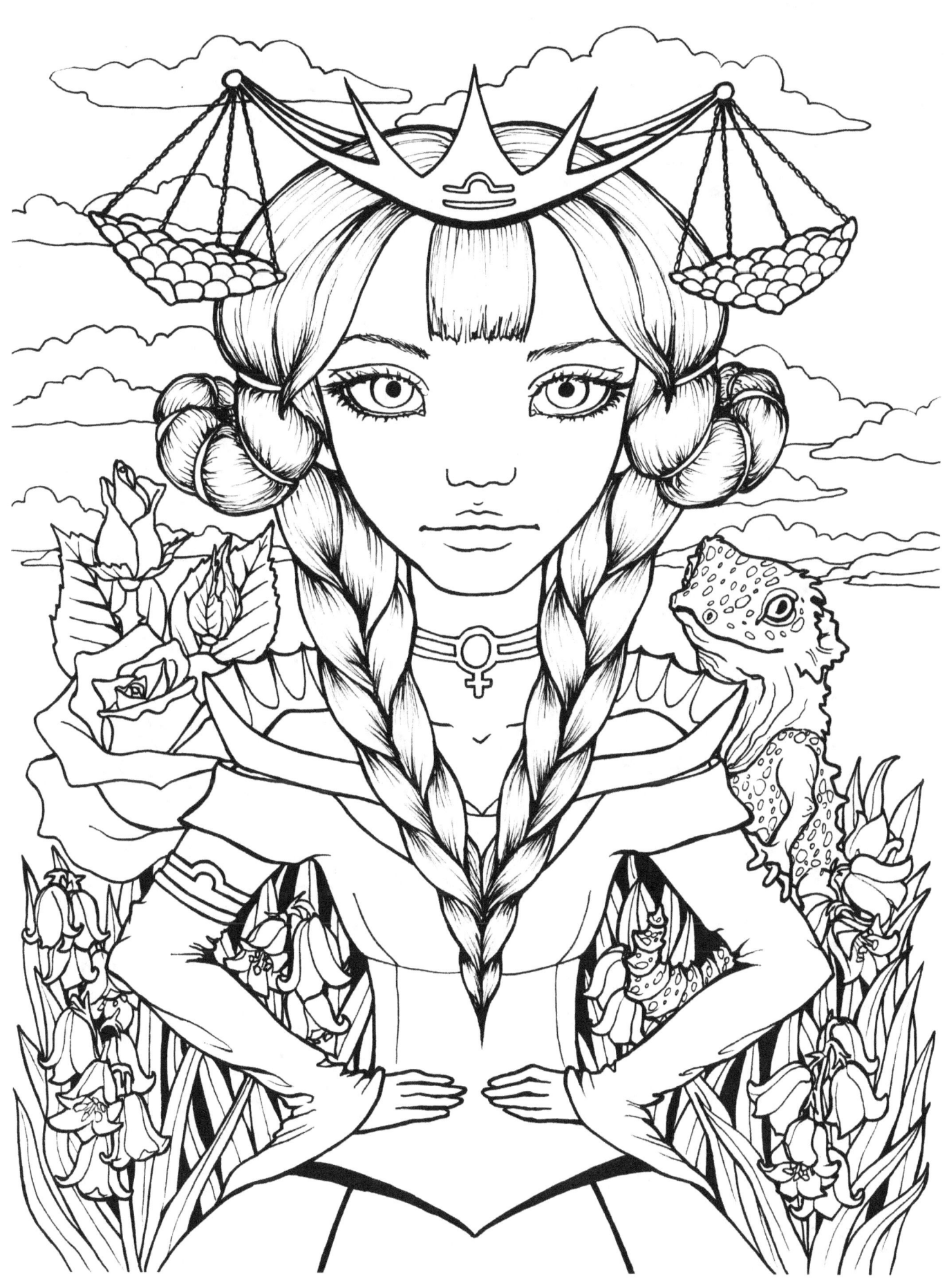

Astro-INKLINGS © Tanya Bond

♎ Libra

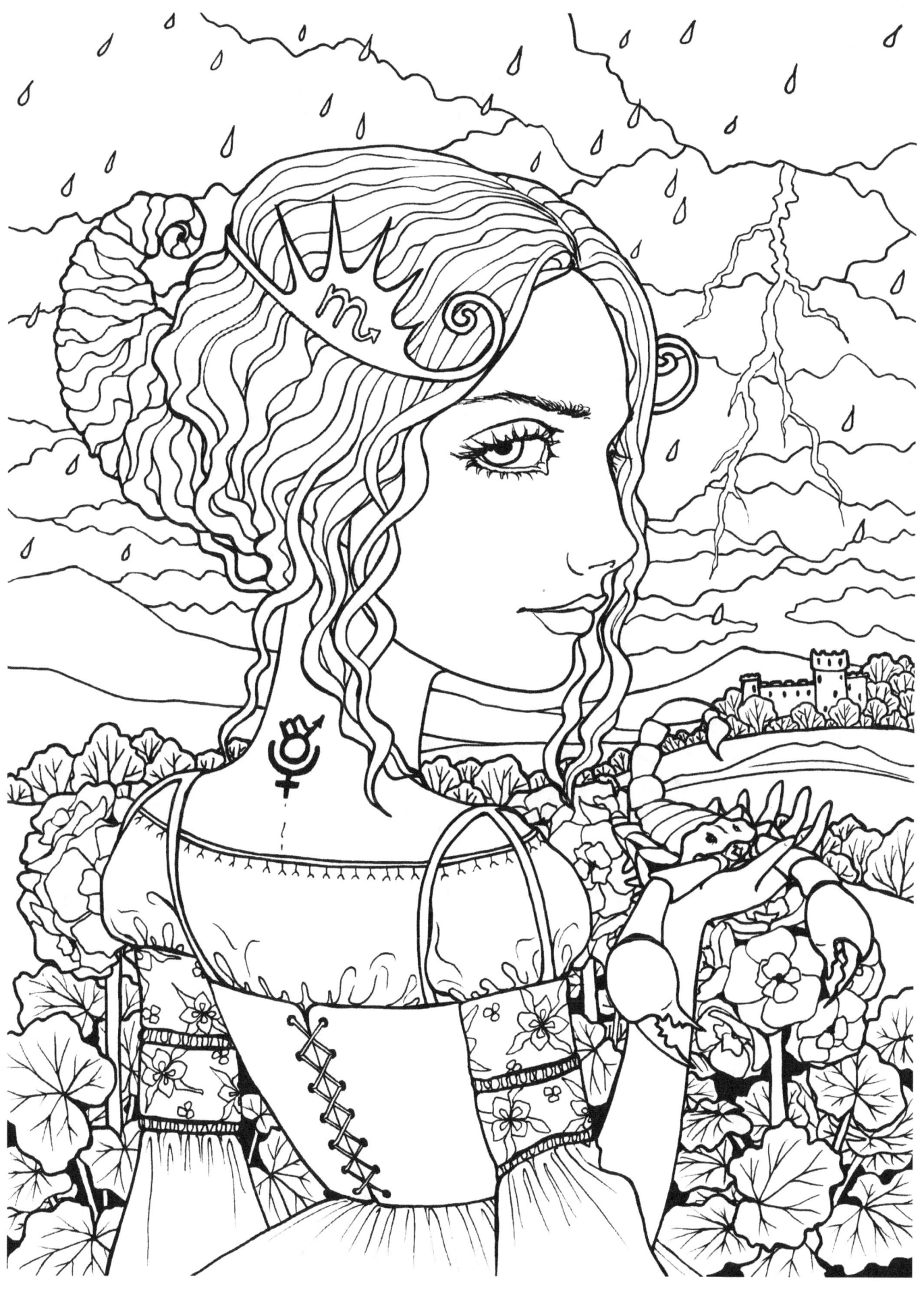

Astro-INKLINGS © Tanya Bond

♏ Scorpio

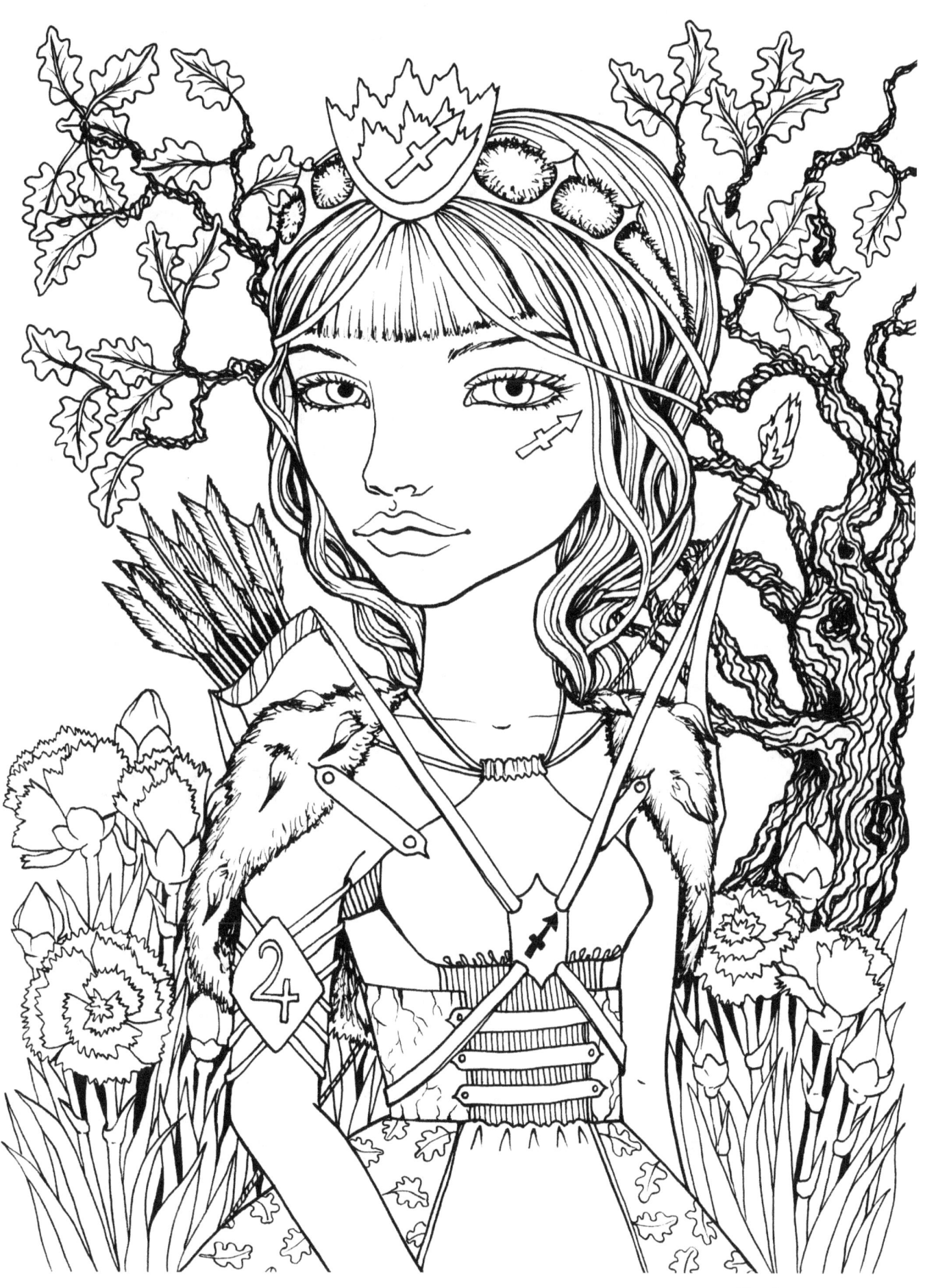

Astro-INKLINGS © Tanya Bond

↗ Sagittarius

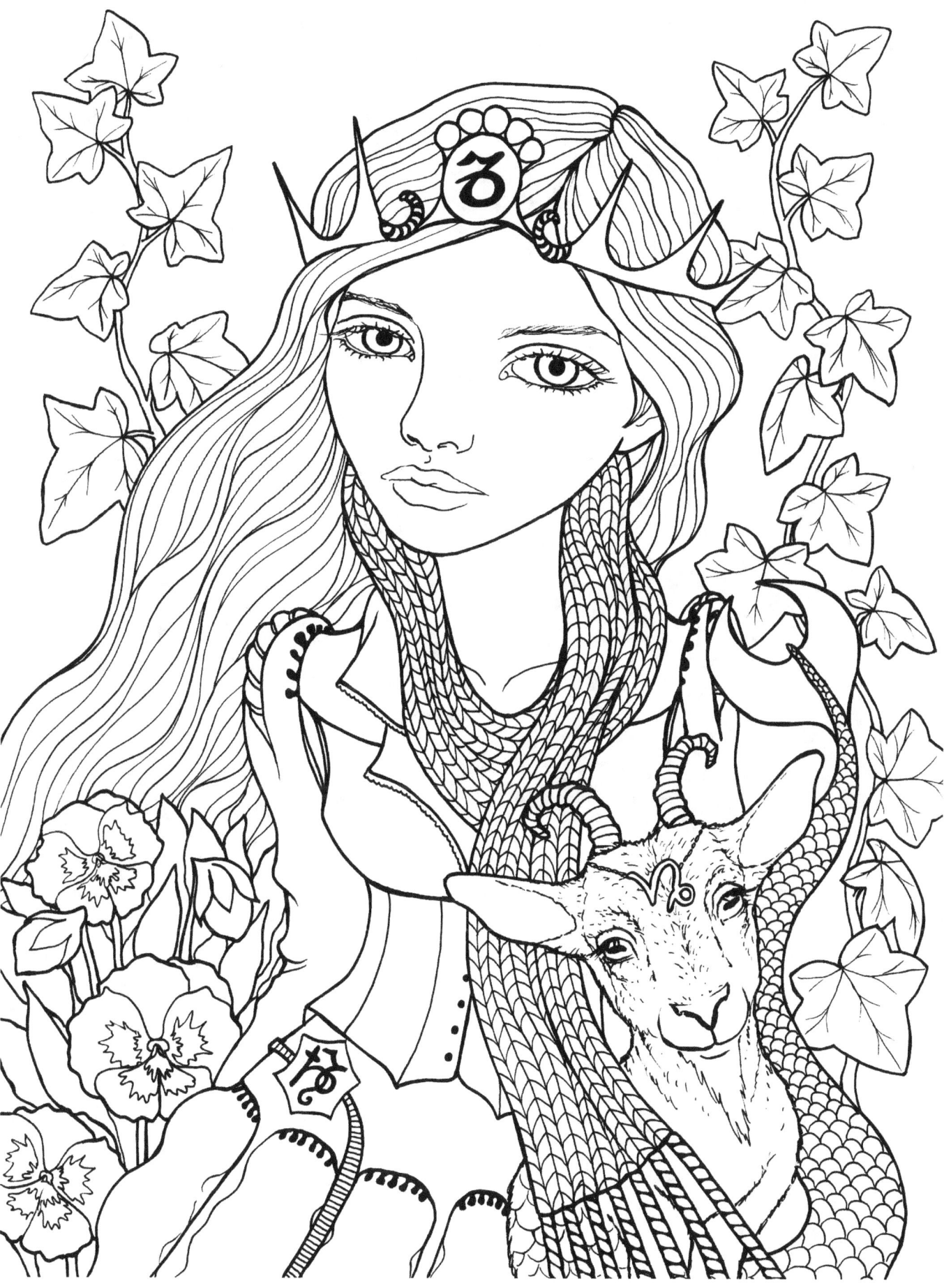

Astro-INKLINGS © Tanya Bond

♑ Capricorn

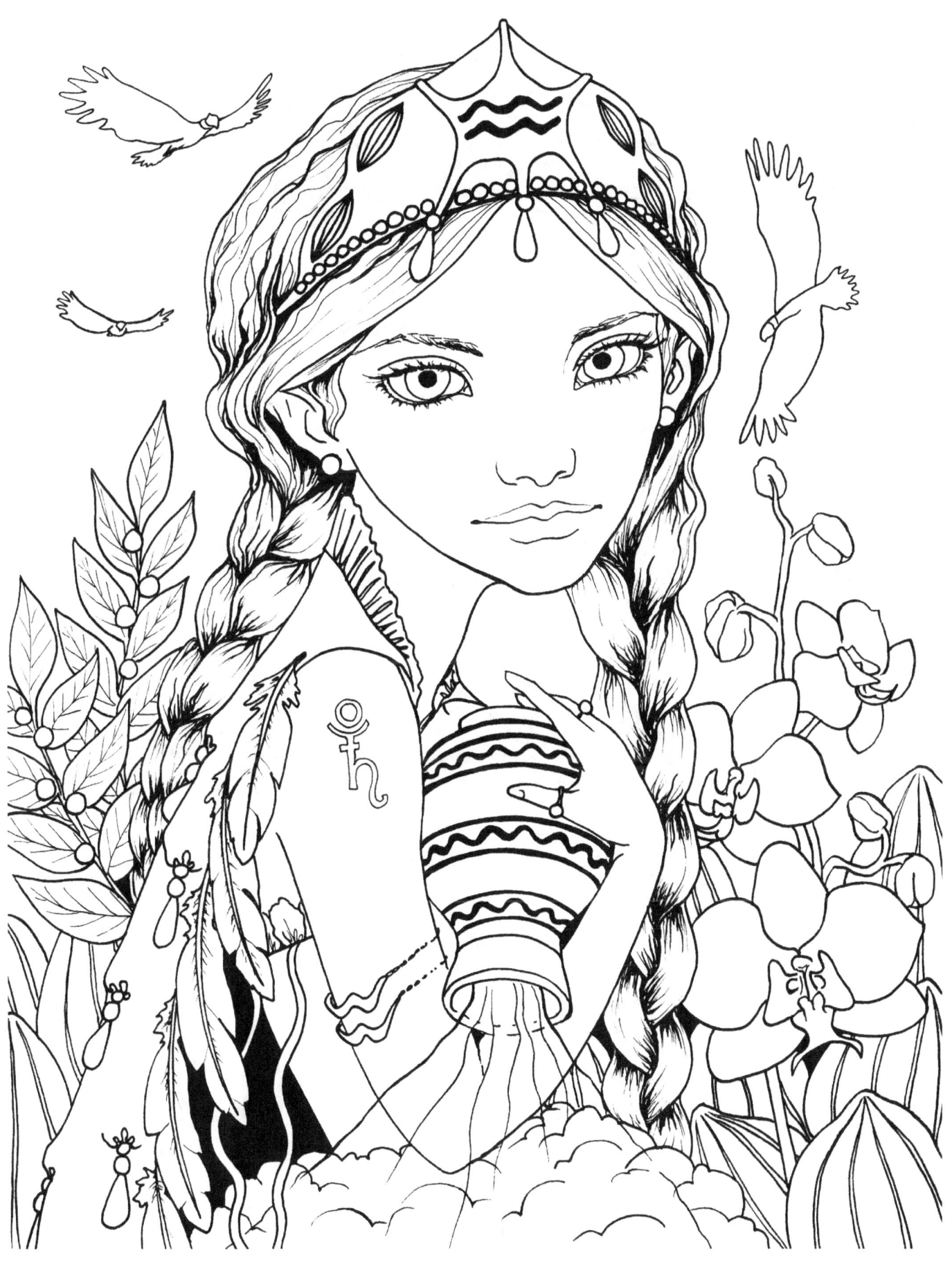

Astro-INKLINGS © Tanya Bond

♒ Aquarius

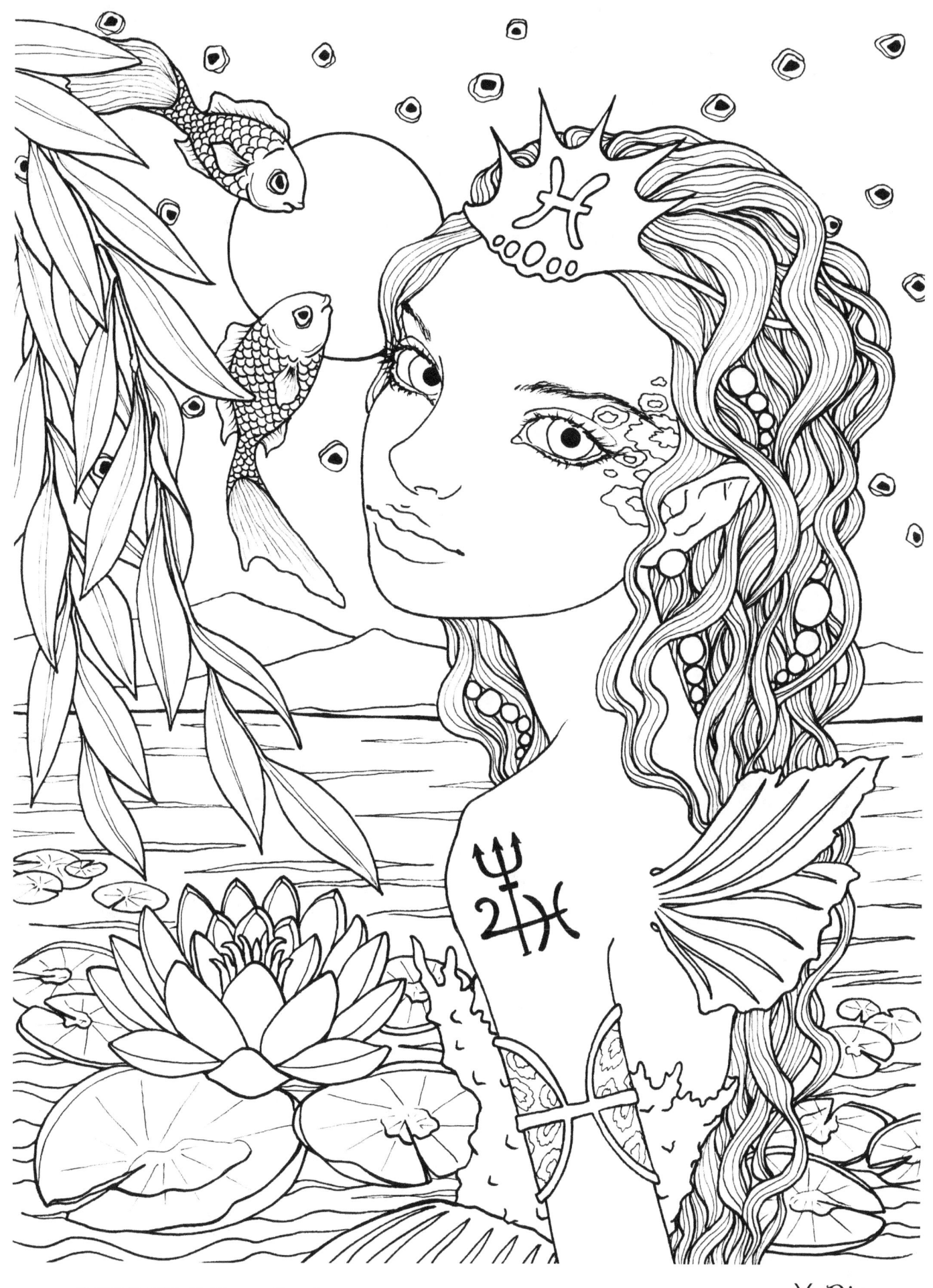

Astro-INKLINGS © Tanya Bond

♓ Pisces

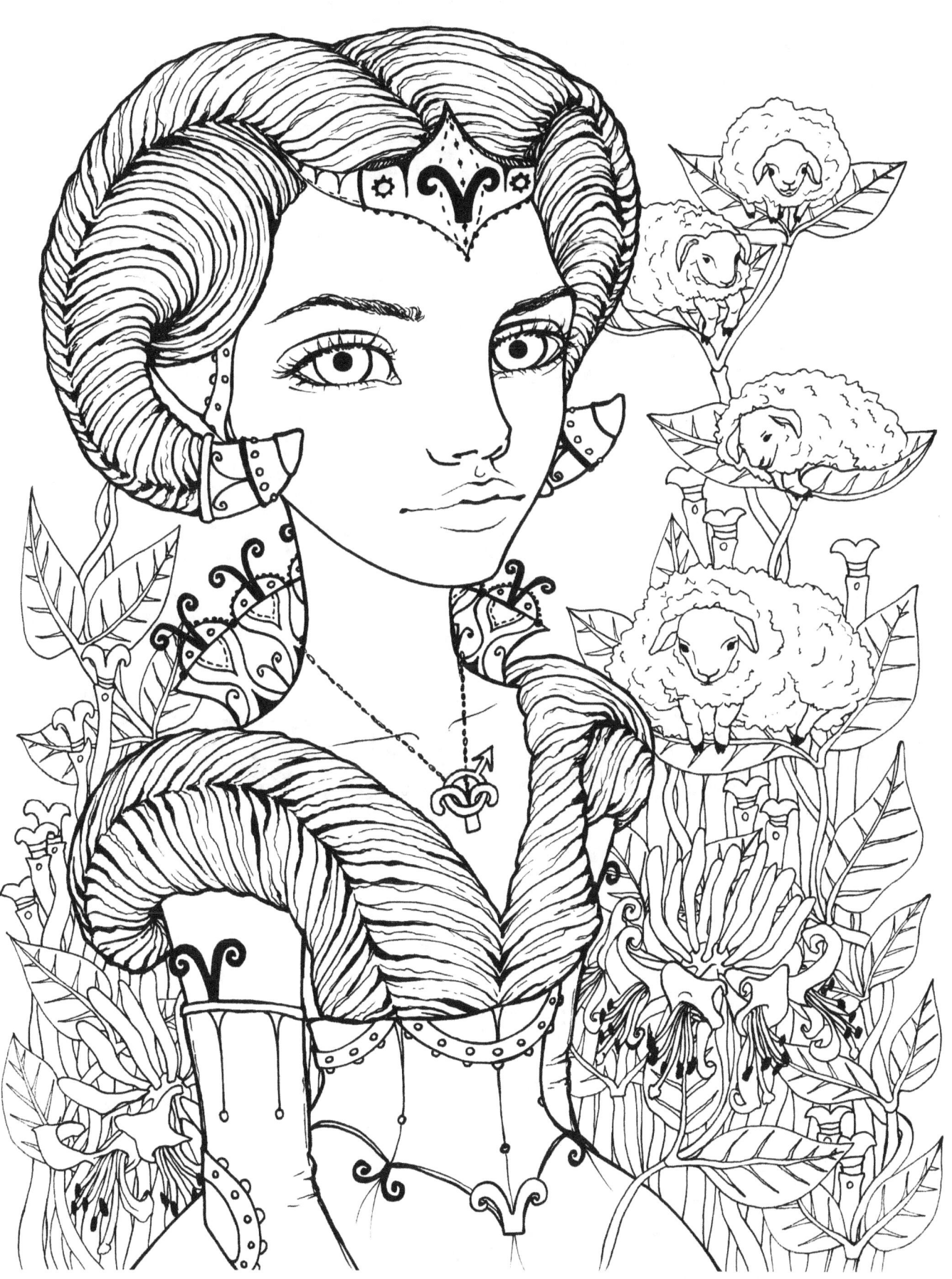

Astro-INKLINGS © Tanya Bond

♈ Aries

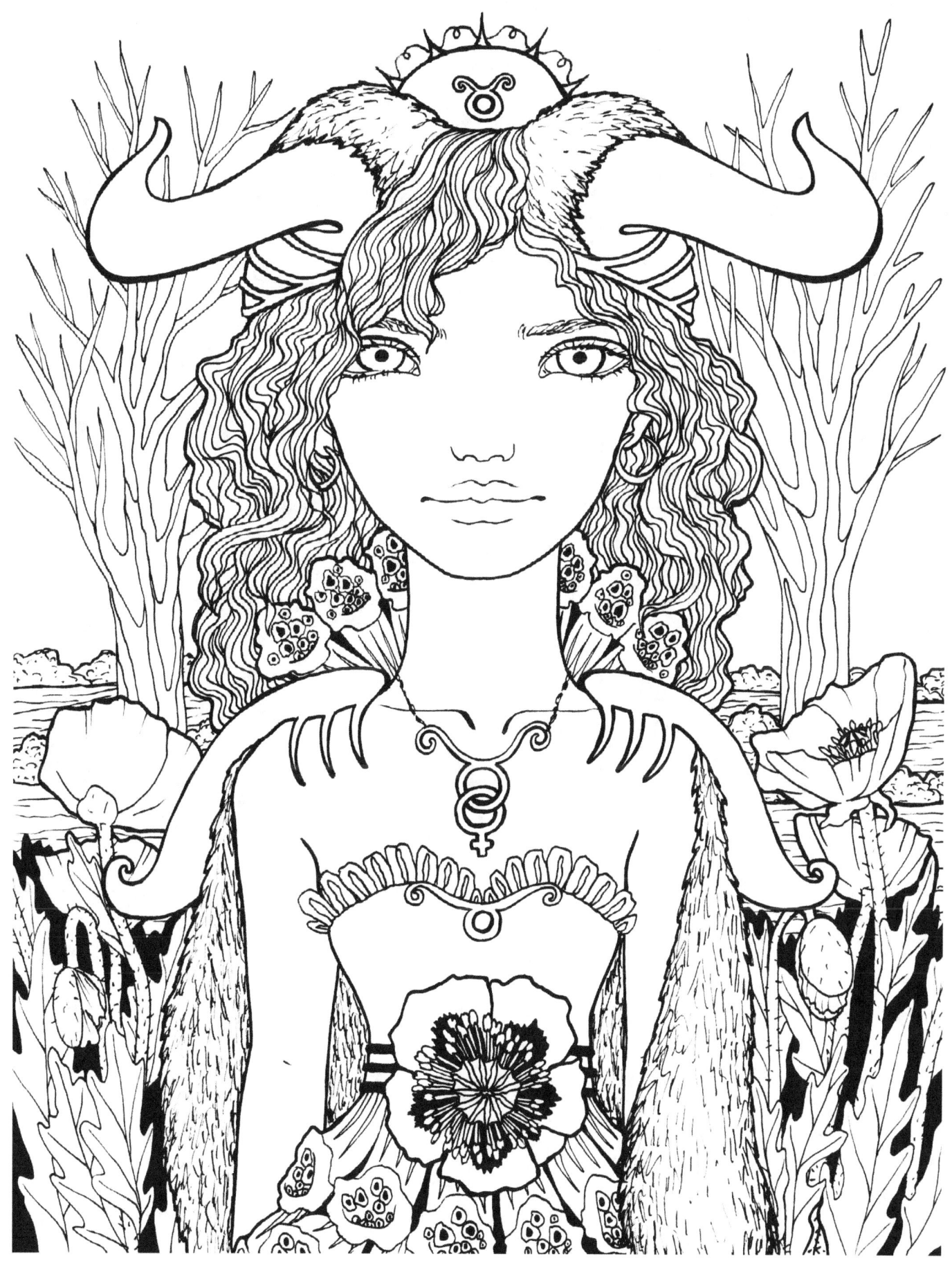

Astro-INKLINGS © Tanya Bond

♉ Taurus

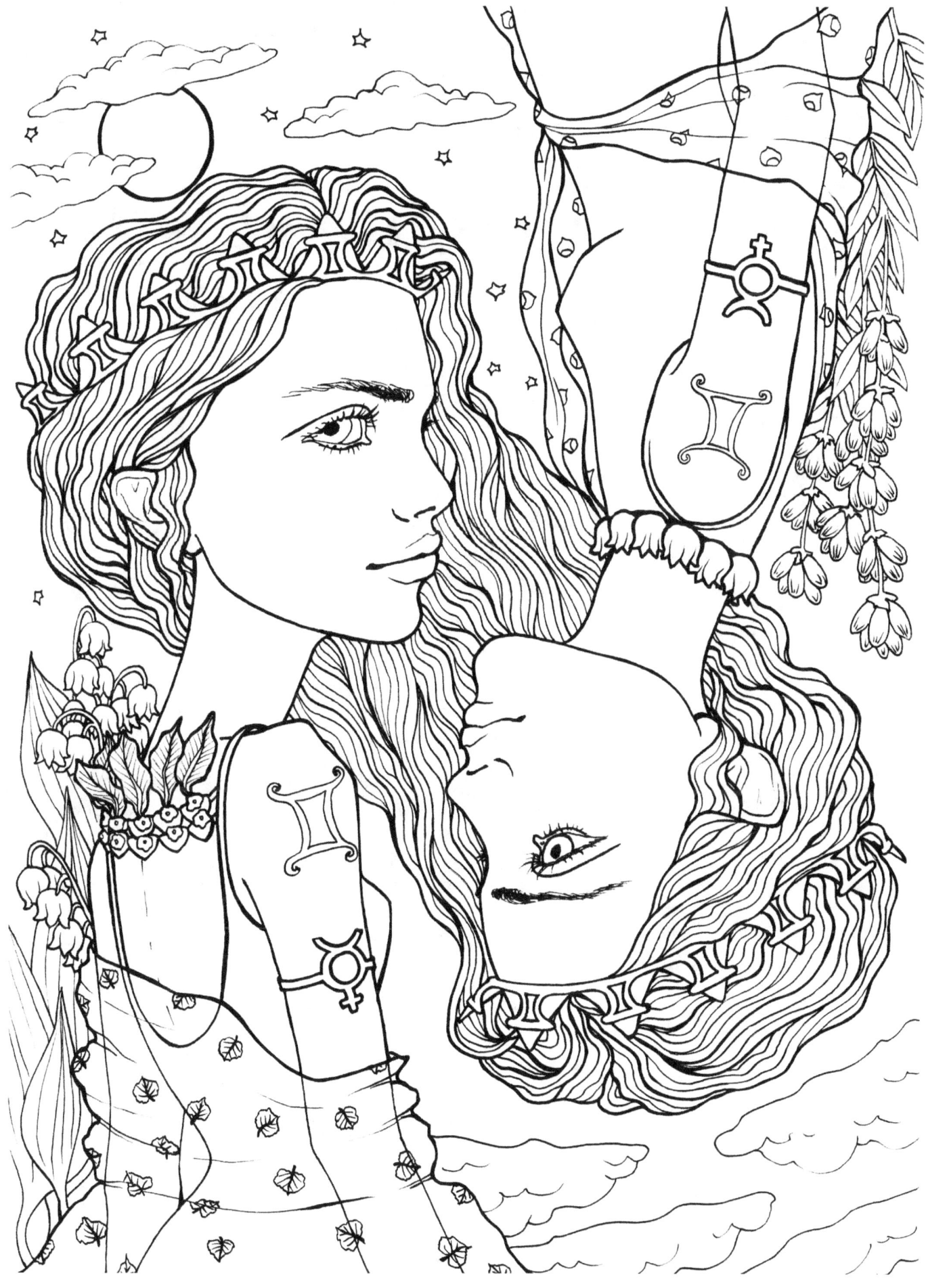

Astro-INKLINGS © Tanya Bond

Ⅱ Gemini

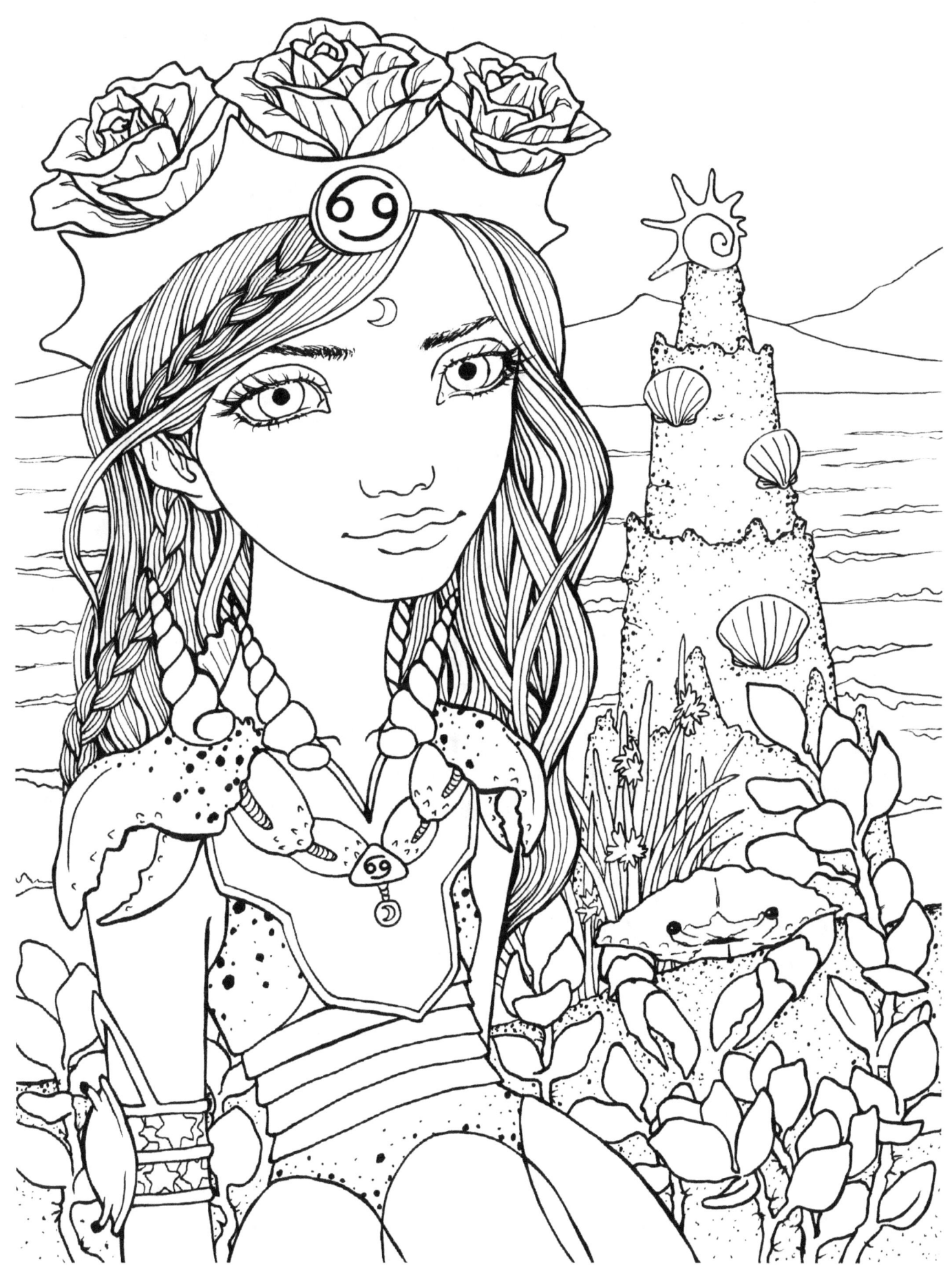

Astro-INKLINGS © Tanya Bond

♋ Cancer

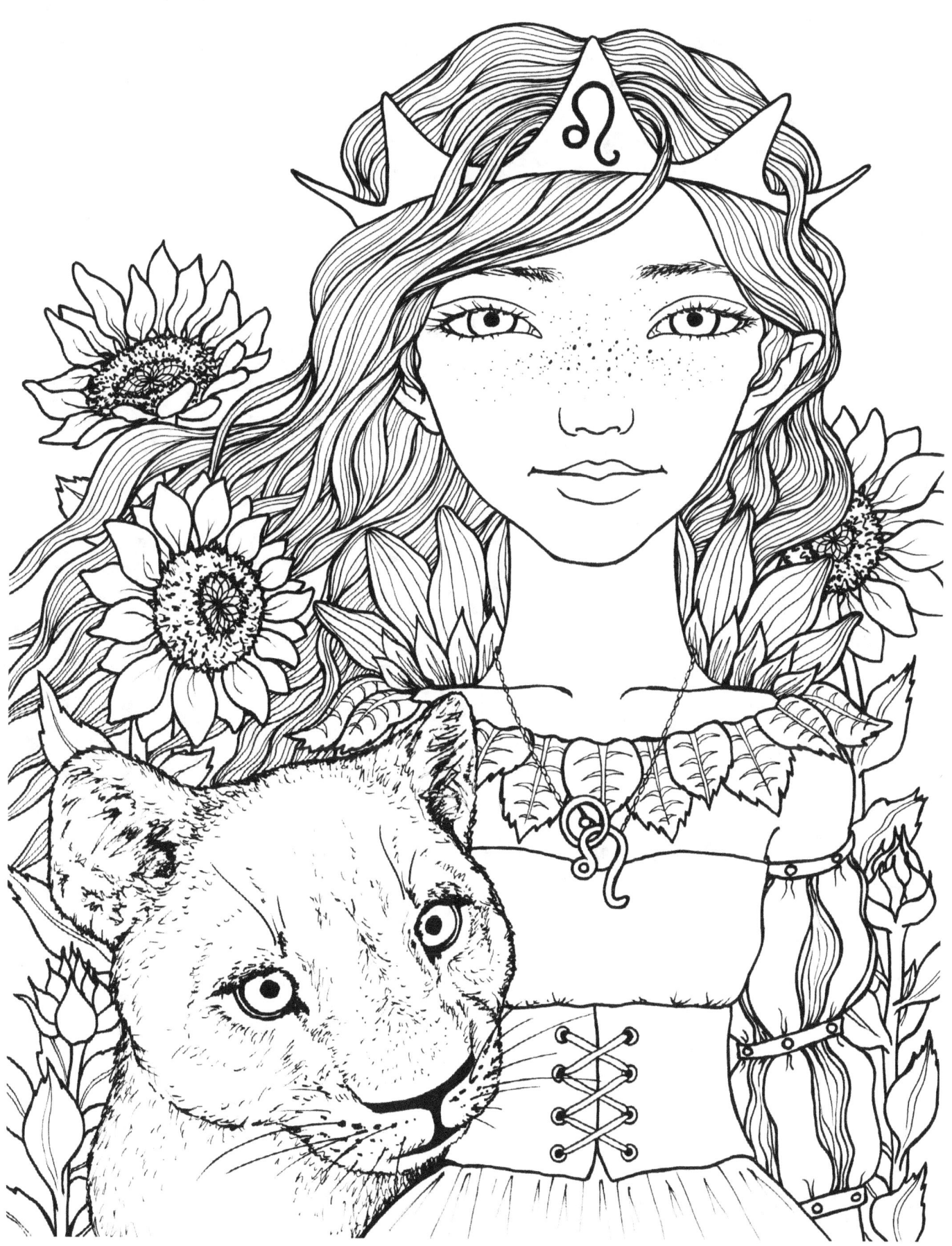

Astro-INKLINGS © Tanya Bond

♌ Leo

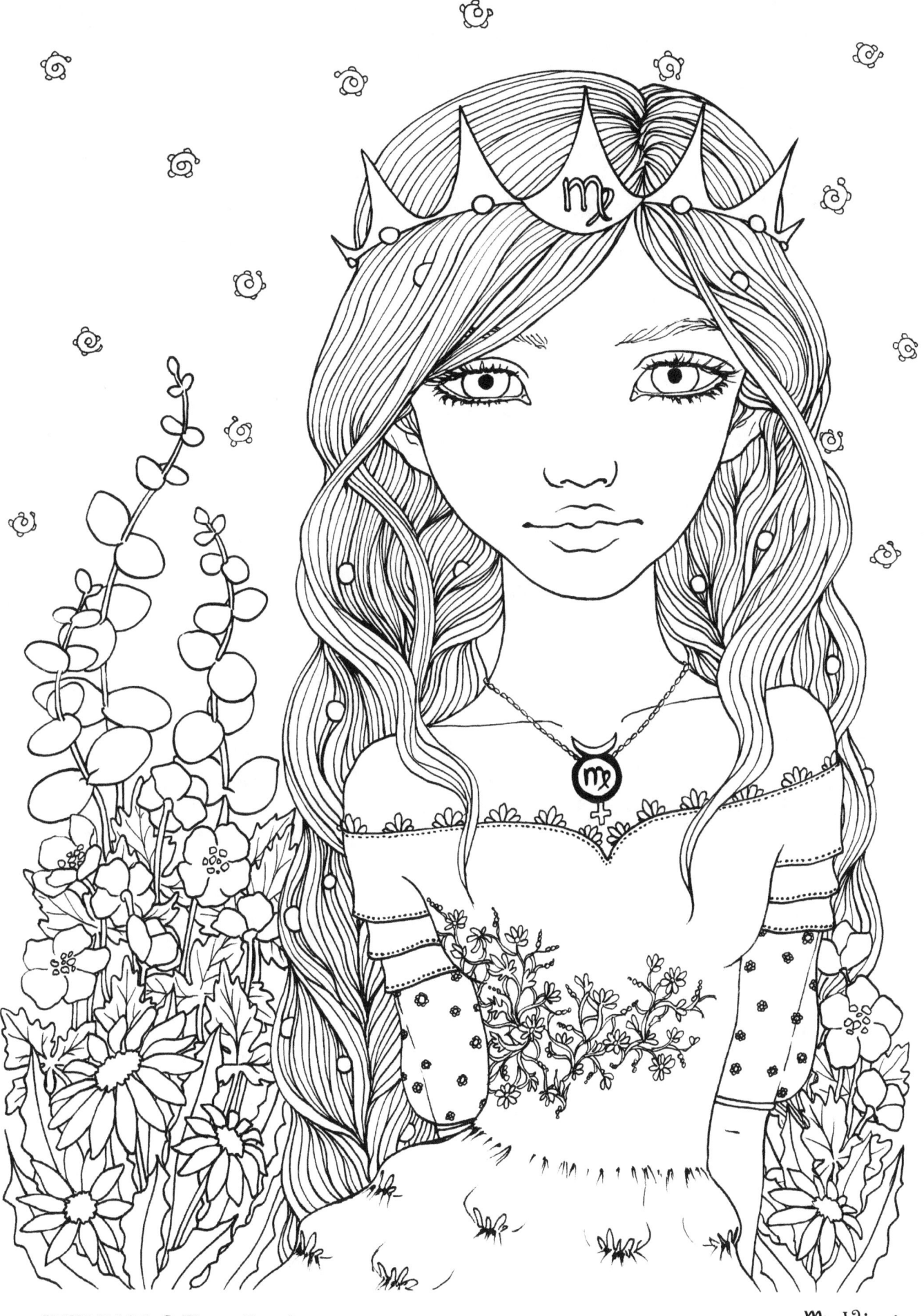

♍ Virgo

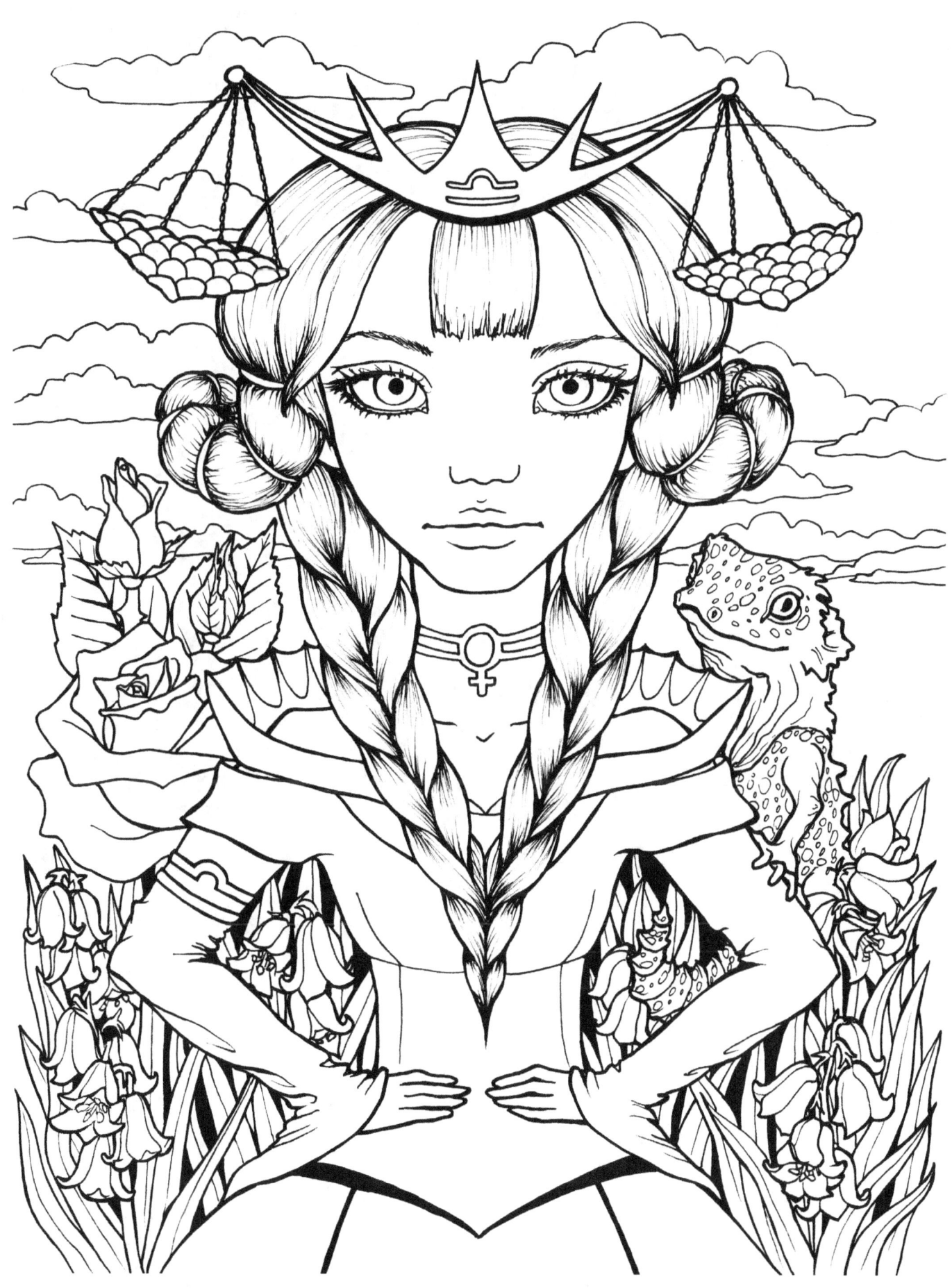

Astro-INKLINGS © Tanya Bond

♎ Libra

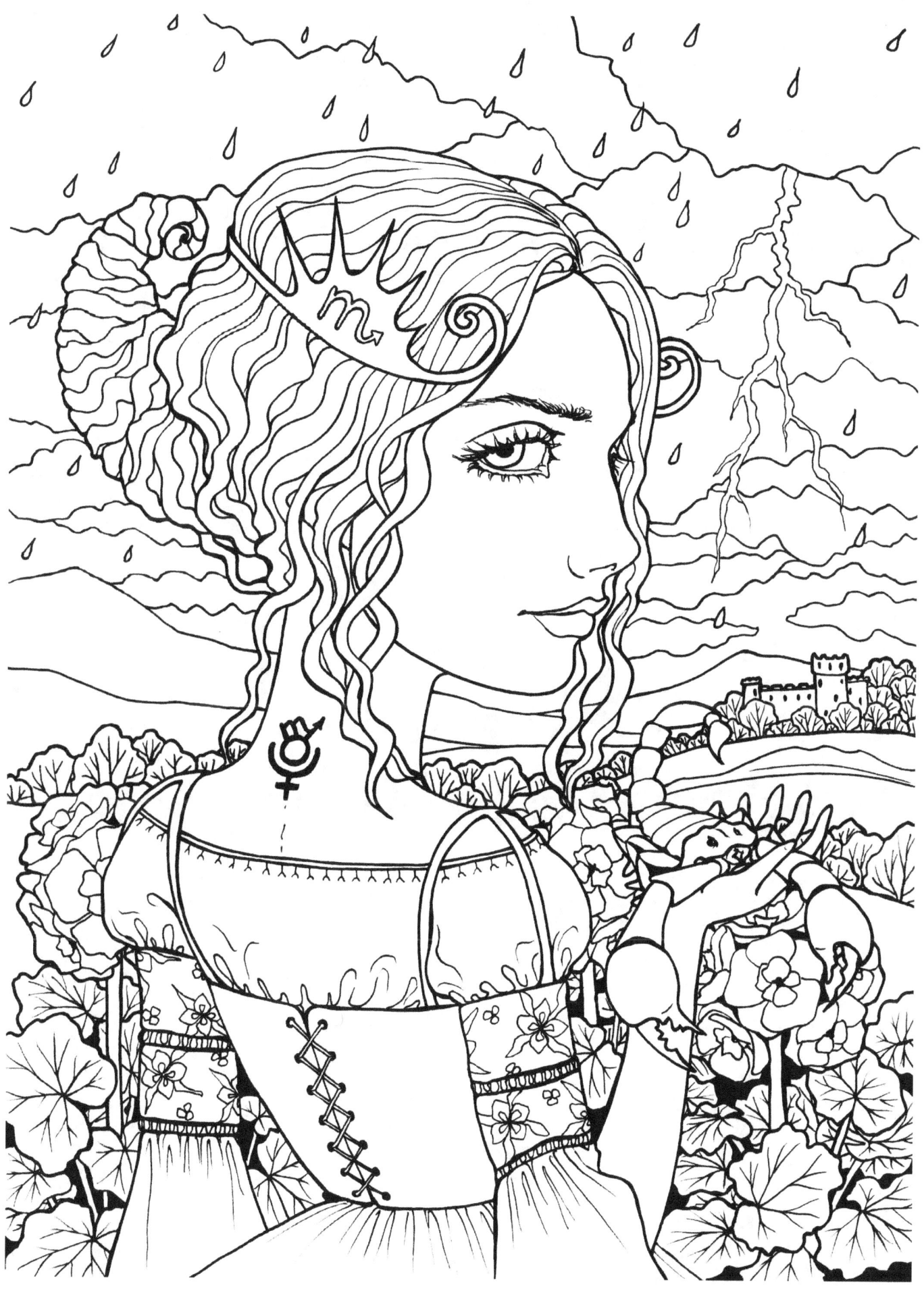

Astro-INKLINGS © Tanya Bond

♏ Scorpio

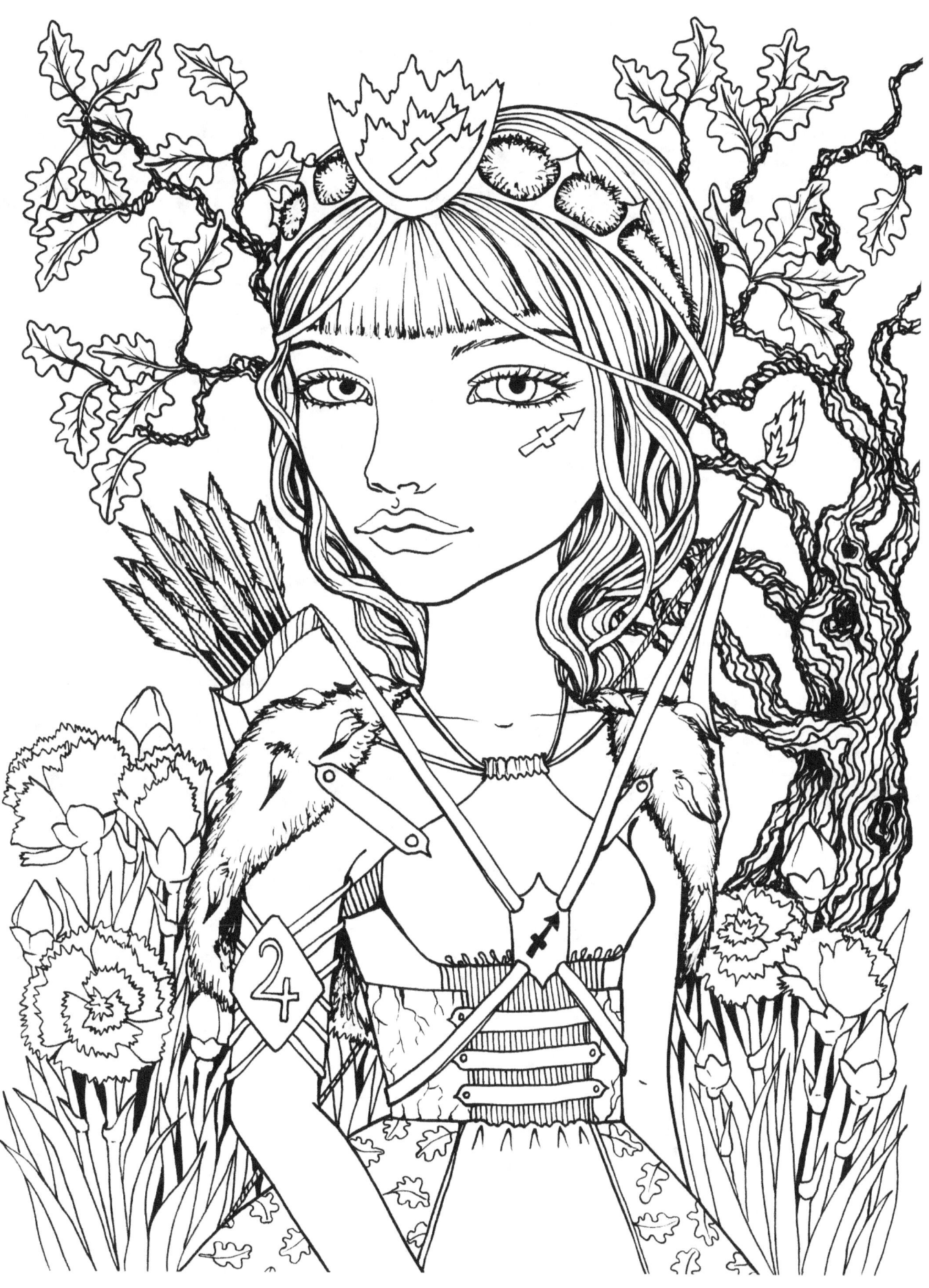

Astro-INKLINGS © Tanya Bond

↗ Sagittarius

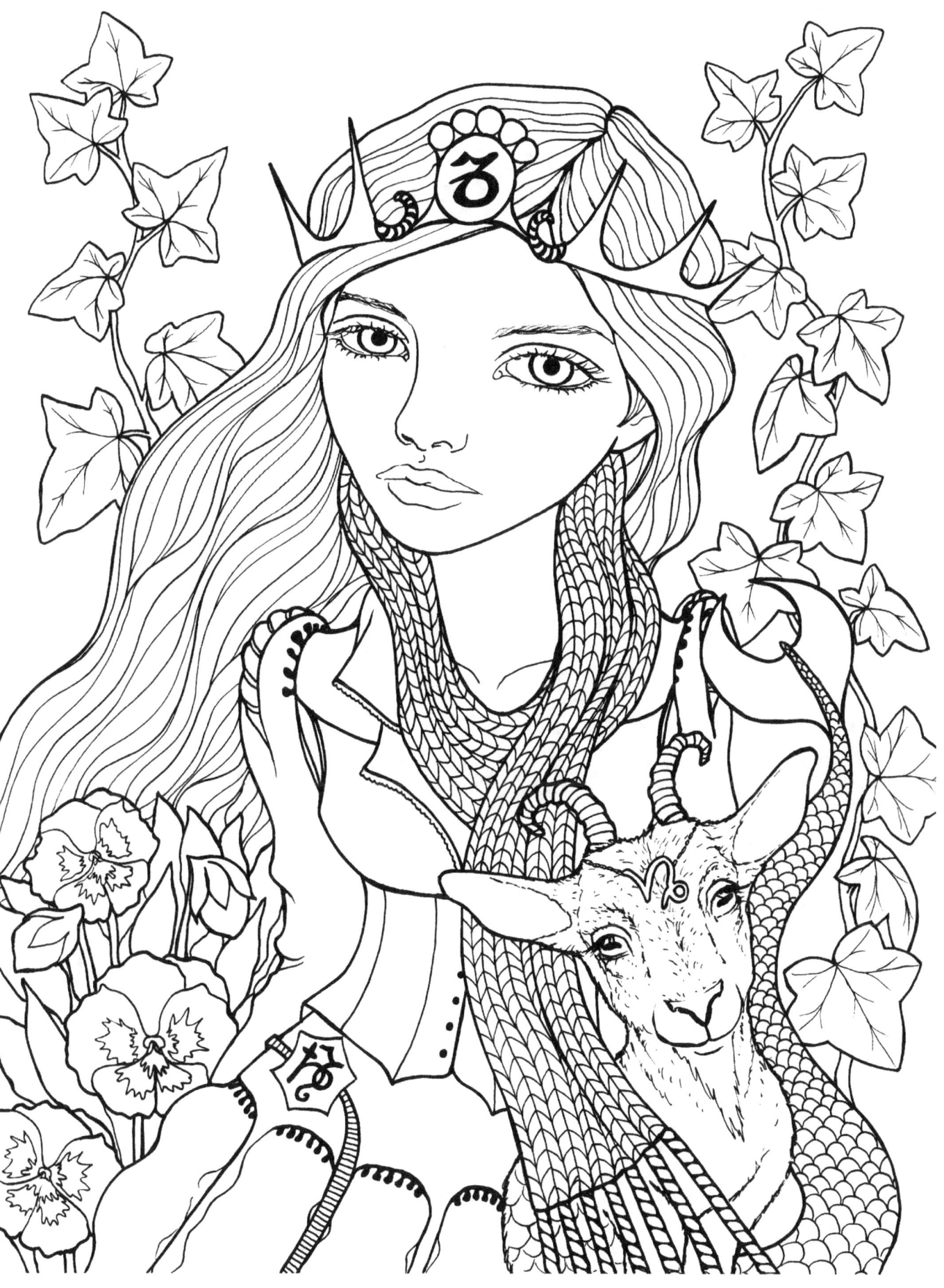

Astro-INKLINGS © Tanya Bond

♑ Capricorn

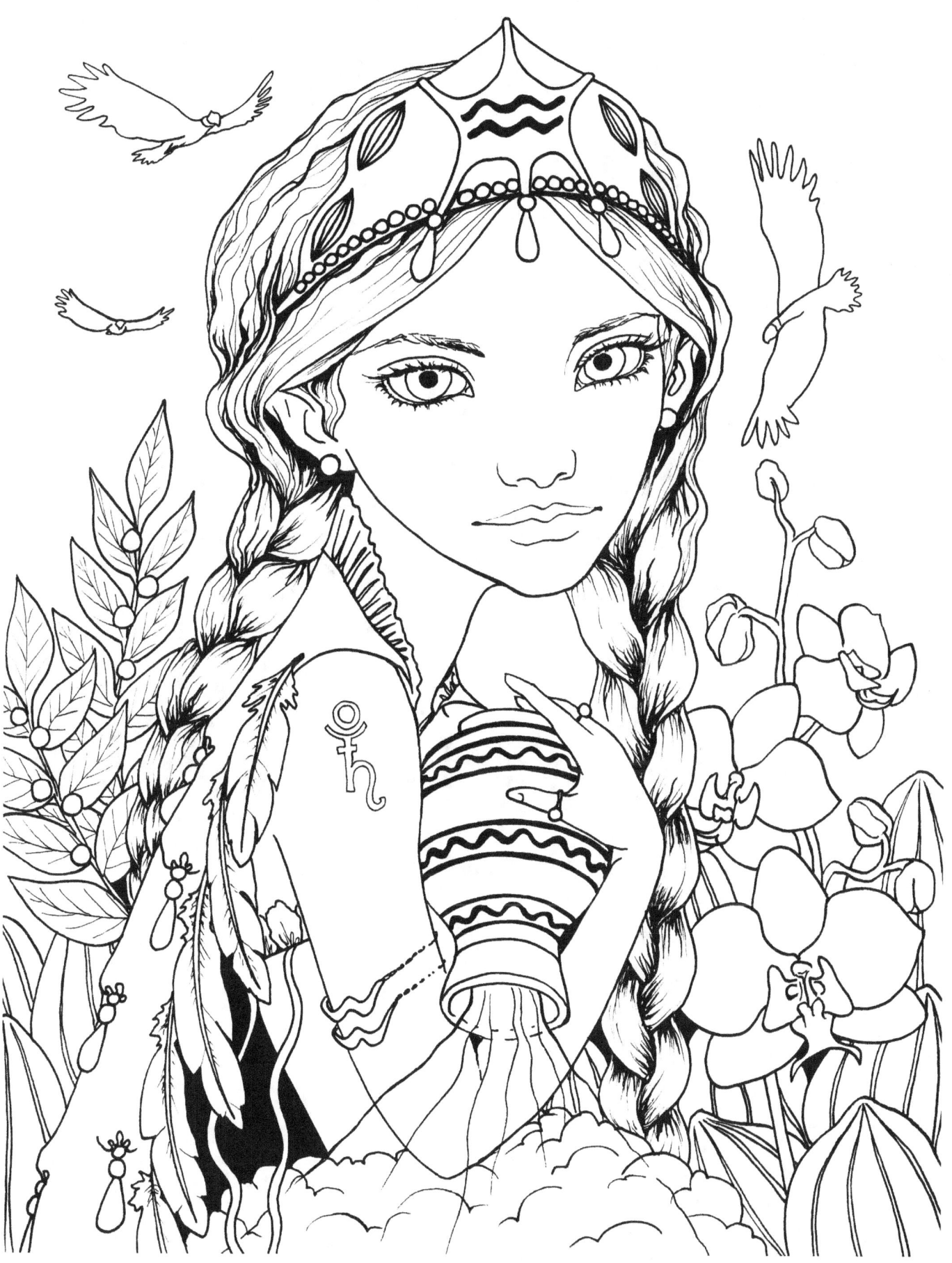

Astro-INKLINGS © Tanya Bond

♒ Aquarius

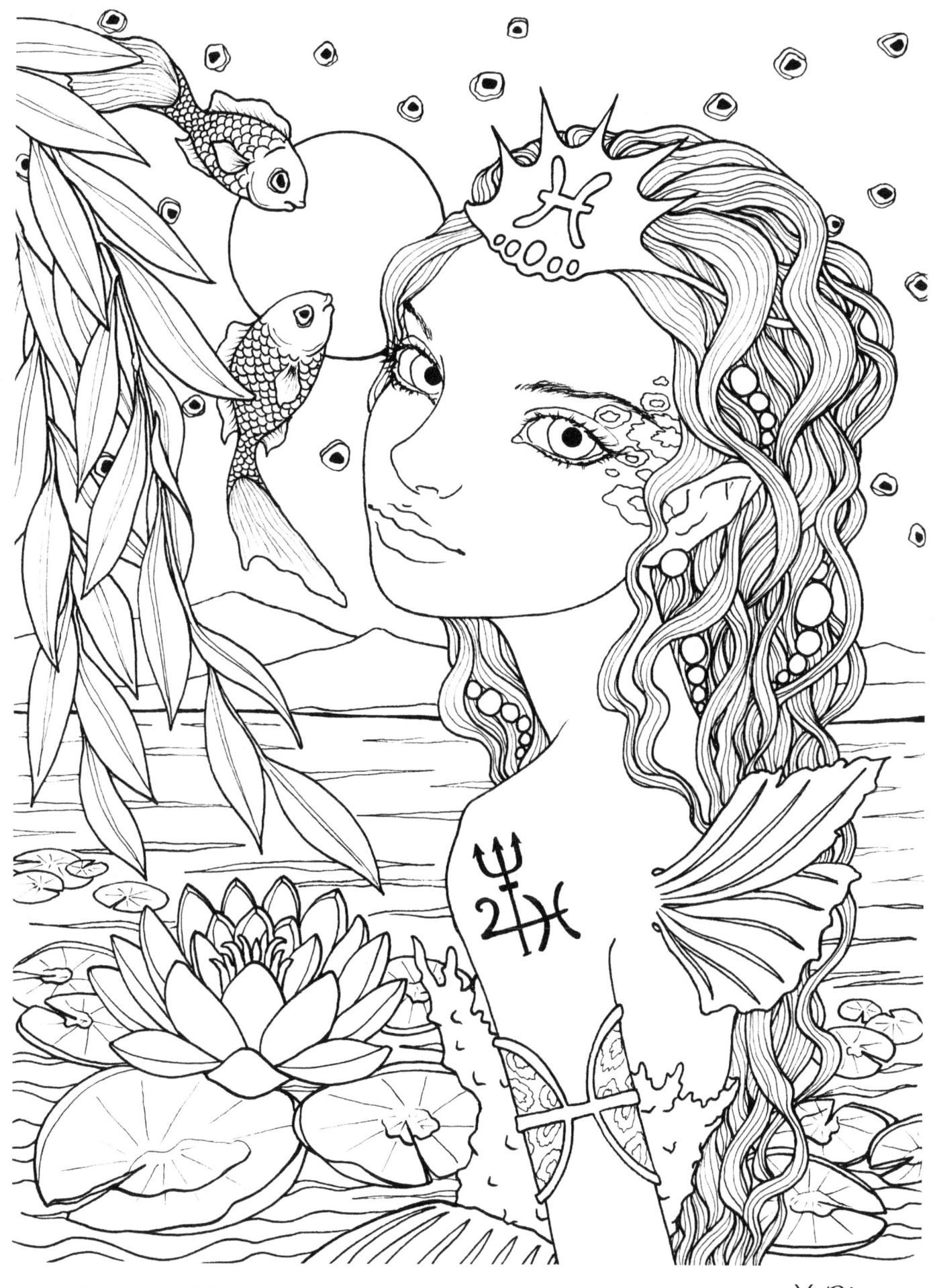

Astro-INKLINGS © Tanya Bond

♓ Pisces

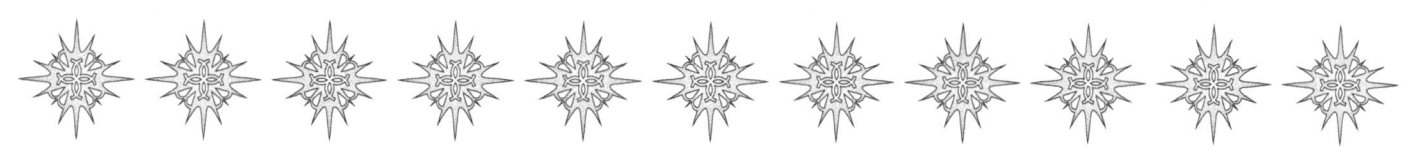

## About the Artist

Tanya Bond is a contemporary artist who creates her charming creatures in beautiful Irish Midlands. In her portraits Tanya strives to capture emotion and hopes to invite the viewer's imagination into the untold stories of her characters.

This is Tanya's fourth colouring book in INKLINGS series.

The illustrations that you find in this book were created in 2016.

You can find Tanya's art on her facebook page where she regularly shares her paintings and drawings, works in progress and new creative ideas - https://www.facebook.com/TanyasCharmingCreatures

You can also find Tanya's work in her Etsy shop
www.tanyabond.com

and on RedBubble
http://www.redbubble.com/people/tanyabond

Thank you for joining the Astro-INKLINGS colouring adventure!

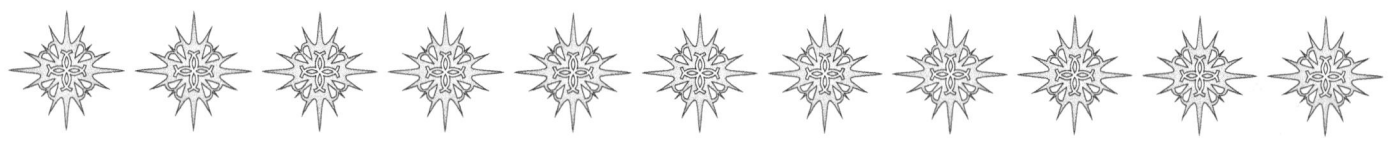

www.ingramcontent.com/pod-product-compliance
Lightning Source LLC
Chambersburg PA
CBHW081132180526
45170CB00008B/3076